THE WAY WE LIVE

with colour

STAFFORD CLIFF

THE WAY WE LIVE

with

colour

WITH COLOUR PHOTOGRAPHS BY

GILLES DE CHABANEIX

Thames & Hudson

THE WAY WE LIVE
with colour

INTRODUCTION 8

1

MONOCHROME COOL 24
Whites and Greys through to Black

2

BLUE-ISH MOODS 68
Indigo to Mauves and Violets

3

RICH REDS AND PALE PINKS 110
Colours of Luxury

4

SUNLIT CITRUS 158
Lemon, Lime and the Alfresco Look

5

NATURALS AND NEUTRALS 194
Beige, Cream and Earth Colours

INDEX 254

Acknowledgments 256

Half-title
Orange on blue: strong colours in the natural world provide inspiration for painters' and decorators' palettes.

Frontispiece
More natural inspiration: blossom flames along a country road in Mauritius.

Title page and Contents page
Vibrant colour gleams on a façade in the bright, hard light of San Cristobal de las Casas, in the Chiapas region of Mexico.

p.4
Cherries provide a highlight of natural colour on the earthy pigments of a ceramic designer's dish.

This page
Markets are rich in colour, as well as texture, form and pattern; food stalls make their effect by the richness of their displays, like this wealth of tomatoes in Mauritius.

Nature creates the same impact: poppies
bloom brightly in the benevolent environment
of a Provence field (*above*).

INTRODUCTION

The orange colour of a tangerine makes a brilliant impact against a background of cobalt blue; in intense sunlight brightly painted Mexican exteriors or Mauritian flame trees acquire additional strength of colour in their assertive reds and pinks; wild poppies in bloom in a field in Provence are a symbolic presence against the surrounding foliage; and in markets the world over the display of fruit, vegetables and, especially, flowers brings visual excitement to our lives. The power of such images in attracting attention suggests that of all the constituent elements of the world around us – forms, textures, sounds and colours – it is the latter which most directly affect our moods and general well-being. And especially in interior design, colour has the most powerful, the most affective, and perhaps the most mysterious influence.

In the fashion industry, there are consultants who can tell you what colour suits your skin tones, your hair, your personality, and so on. But it is in our own homes, where we express our lifestyle choices in decoration and furnishings, that colours have the most direct effect on our emotions – making us feel happy or sad, relaxed or energetic. Certain colours seem to create specific sensations: blue is good for bedrooms (calming); yellow for bathrooms (wake-up), red for kitchens, and an entire rainbow for children's rooms. And that is only the start – there are also shades of colour that soften or accelerate those reactions. There is a very big difference between a pale, creamy pink – and fuchsia. Even some of the terms used for colours say something about their emotional associations: sky blue, buttercup yellow, slate grey, arctic white, for instance.

Such names are often the creations of paint manufacturers in which we also participate. Then we may consider the results of using colours together: blue and white, orange and yellow, red and green, or perhaps that should be expressed as 'geranium and lime', or 'flame and leaf'. Colour has a powerful way of evoking whole ranges of associations – a favourite football team, perhaps, or a slice of Battenburg cake. It can also evoke historic periods and styles – Art Nouveau, Art Deco, wartime austerity, or the Sixties. Certain shades of cream and dark green in a kitchen can evoke pre-World War II gloom, while grey and white may feel sophisticated and modern.

As its series title implies, this book is mainly concerned with the intimate and personal use of colour, but it also recognizes the debt we owe to the natural world and to the random or deliberate effects of colours applied to urban or rural exteriors. The photographs in the chapters that follow are part of the remarkable archive of the late Gilles de Chabaneix, a photographer who travelled the world and spent over twenty-five years observing and capturing life. He was expert at snapping inspiration wherever he saw it; his eye for colour and composition was incomparable. From the street market to the rooftops, from the most humble house to the palace, from the tiniest detail to the broadest vista, he captured the colours of everyday life, both interior and exterior. Here, they are arranged in the form of an inspirational sourcebook.

Our selection of the photographs led us to identify five major groupings. First, the monochrome, in which white, black and neutral shades of grey are either used for their own distinctive qualities or as backgrounds for splashes of more assertive colours. In the blues, we have an opportunity of observing how colour can be used to create a particular 'feel', and how, combined with white, it can express a whole culture – that of the Mediterranean. Reds and pinks appear as the colours of luxury and fine living. Yellows and greens bring the sun and natural light into the interior. And a final grouping looks at those colours which seem to be principally derived from natural materials.

The natural world is, indeed, a great teacher. Painting a room bright green can create a shock effect, but so can a green vase in an all-white room, or a bright pink bloom against a grey or a blue wall. Some of the pictures in these pages rely for their impact simply on the colour from a slice of watermelon or a single strawberry. It doesn't even have to be a bright colour; a whole room of beige, cream, tan and taupe can be as powerful a mood creator as a blue rollerblind or a red rug. Some people say they want a blue and white kitchen, or an all-grey living room, but others are less certain. 'I just want a change', or 'I only know when I see it', is a common response. So that's where this book comes to the rescue. Try painting just a patch of wall initially. Look at the colour in different light; at night, when it's raining. Good colour choices don't rely on sunlight. If it's fabric for curtains or blinds – pin up a swatch; if it's a sofa, consider a big bright cushion or a loose cover. Give yourself the flexibility to have fun. Finally, don't forget the contribution that people themselves make to a room: their clothes, their books, their toys. A successful colour scheme is one that makes people feel comfortable too. And that brings us back again to the question of colour and feeling – and that is entirely up to you.

Colour does not need to be bright to be effective. Relative lack of colour – as observable on the monochromatic façades of these preserved structures in New York State (*left above* and *below*) – has the effect of focusing attention on details of form and texture rather than on external decoration.

Snow in a Slovakian winter creates a dramatic black-and-white effect (*right above*). A similar colour scheme is created by paint alone on one of the traditional villas of San Francisco (*right below*).

AUSTRALIA

SLOVAKIA

Sombre tones, again, like monochromatic treatments, allow detail to assert itself, from body painting by indigenous Australians to the variations of surface on buildings and objects (*left*).

A similarly restrained palette has been observed by the owners of this house in Marrakesh (*opposite*), where visual interest is created by the careful positioning of small objects, including a group of traditional hats.

Overleaf
The greys and greens of surface patinas, as well as parts of the animal kingdom, form an inspiring, natural colour range.

GRANADA

PARIS

Blues are ubiquitous in their various shades: indigos, cobalts, ultramarines suggest a purity and cleanliness, most often associated with coastal communities where the colour may define aspects of national style, as with this burnous wearer from the Berber tribe of 'blue' men in Marrakesh (*left*) or in these varied locations (*opposite*). In the island setting of Sri Lanka blues and greys of the sea and land are emblematic of a life surrounded by colour (*overleaf*).

CHAPTER 1

MONOCHROME COOL

Whites and Greys, through to Black

This first section might almost be regarded as concerning itself with the absence of colour rather than with the positive application of pigment. However, the very reticence and understatement of many of the examples illustrated here becomes a positive factor in that they provide the ideal background for the display of colourful or complex artifacts and furniture. Other interiors make a distinct minimalist statement out of the use of single, non-assertive colour to achieve a classical, modernist elegance.

Black and white: the natural and the man-made combine to stark effect on a church in Quebec, Canada (*opposite*).

The shapes of footprints in the sand make a pattern in a seemingly colourless situation that nonetheless creates an iconic image, evoking the simple and sensual pleasures of life at the water's edge (*this page*).

NEPAL

RHODES

Surface detail in the form of window and door surrounds makes itself noticed through the absence of bright colour (*left*). In some communities, local byelaws may also demand conformity to non-obtrusive colour schemes, as is the case in this preserved village in New York State (*opposite*).

CHILOE

MADRID

White is the coolest of colours, but can still be used positively in a multitude of contexts and locations. It complements the refined elegance of this villa in Istanbul (*above left*); it filters and enhances outside light in a house in Corsica (*above right*); it illuminates and emphasizes intrinsically interesting forms –here, a horse statue in Umbria (*opposite left*) and the Art Nouveau panels of a doorway in Brussels (*opposite right*).

GREECE

BRUSSELS

ISTANBUL

SRI LANKA

STOCKHOLM

AUVERGNE

More examples of surface detail looking intriguing and complex without the distraction of strong colours (*opposite*); similarly, the finely worked doors in a Marrakesh house (*right*) lend a modern quality to a space which is effectively a reworking of the time-honoured Islamic court – a place of restraint and simplicity.

Transitional spaces, such as stair-wells, passages and corridors, are frequently starved of natural light, yet they are central to the proper functioning of any living space. In such cases, the use of pale, monochromatic colour schemes is entirely appropriate, not only because of their lightening effect, but also because such walls make marvellous display areas for works of art: in a Brussels apartment (*above left*); in a farmhouse near Bologna (*above right*); in a traditional house on the Greek island of Mykonos (*opposite left*); and in another Brussels apartment (*opposite right*).

The subtle interplay of outside light
and interior shade, fundamental
to the charms of this Marrakesh
house (*above*), is furthered by the
use of restrained colour schemes
in the inner rooms that give on to
the central courtyard. The room is
given a more contemporary feel by
the painting of the wooden shutters.

In this elegant Paris interior (*above*) a pale colour scheme – including the floor – comes into its own as the most effective background for the display of objects and furniture, emphasizing the simple lines of the furniture in chinoiserie style.

Pale grey-greens and whites allow the magnificent proportions of a first-floor apartment in a seventeenth-century house in Versailles to speak for themselves (*this page* and *opposite*). The reticence of the decoration in all the rooms allows the forms of the furniture to assume greater importance. Mixed with the lovingly assembled collection of fine pieces – the owner is an interior decorator of international repute – are objects of rougher texture. For instance, the fuel for a wood-burning stove is prominently displayed as much for its look as its usefulness.

Bleached wood and white painted panels have peculiarly coastal connotations, however elaborate the furnishing of an interior may be (*opposite*) – here, in one of the residences of a French restaurateur on the west coast of France. White and grey also seem to be the only appropriate colours for the rough-hewn interiors of a coastal dwelling on the island of Corsica (*left*).

Certain spaces, both interior and exterior, beg for the simplest possible treatment in terms of colour and texture – the case with all these shower installations in very different environments: a coastal house in Corsica (*above left*); a courtyard in Bali (*above right*); a second residence on the Île de Ré (*opposite left*); a traditional Moroccan house (*opposite right*). Though not an obvious choice for a bathroom, the colour grey works well in a variety of styles.

Cool whites and pale yellows create a sense of restrained luxury in the dining-room of a Corsican house (*left*). No jarring elements intrude upon this peaceful scene; even the high backs of the dining chairs have been given a softer look by their loose linen covers, discreetly bordered. All the more dramatic, then, seem the colours of the owner's collection of mounted entomological specimens.

The initially spartan impression
created by the extensive use of
white or off-white in many
modernist interiors can be
successfully countered by the
introduction of softer forms and
fabrics into the decorative scheme.
In the bedroom of this Paris
apartment (*right*) a 'soft' effect
has been achieved by introducing
a tent-like hanging of the white
cotton drapes surrounding the
actual bed area.

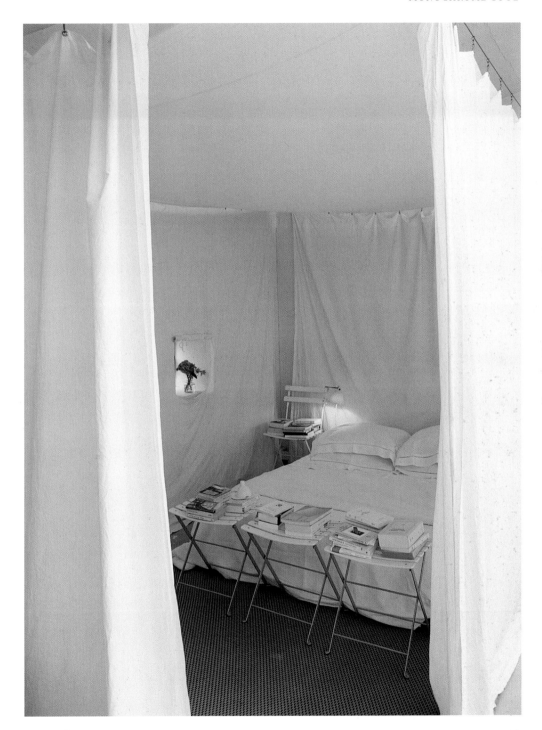

The unobtrusive colours of these fireplaces – in Paris (*above left*), in Brussels (*above right*), in Los Angeles (*opposite left*) and London (*opposite right*) – in rooms with white or near-white walls make them initially less of a point of focus. However, in all these cases, their form and significance within the room have been re-emphasized by the objects placed upon and around them. Both the hearth areas and the chimney breasts have become surfaces for decorative display.

These two interiors, one in New York (*left*) and one in London (*opposite*) both use a restrained palette to create rather different effects. The former exudes an elegant modernism in the distribution of furniture and objects in simple, tidy groupings against a dramatic black-painted floor. In contrast, the owners of the London townhouse have opted for a look which allows the inherited textures of the building's construction to show through in the form of original, untreated floorboards and whitewashed walls.

The owners of this house in Sicily (*preceding pages*) have decided to extend the overall cool look of the interiors to their choice of furniture – simple lines and pale colours, making a perfect background to the display of large-scale works of art. This colour scheme is extended to the other reception rooms of the house and to the kitchen and bedrooms (*above* and *opposite*) through unadorned openings.

The interiors of this house in the Marais district of Paris are unified by a black and white decorative theme (*preceding pages*, *left* and *opposite*). Airy, light rooms are the setting for the owner's eclectic collections of modern and Directoire furniture and of art, including works by Dubuffet, Miro and a range of African art.

The richly sculptural forms of African statuary (*above left*) stand out against the white walls and fitted shelves of the main rooms of the house (*see preceding pages*). In another Paris interior (*above right* and *opposite left*) black and white complement each other in a whole range of vignettes and detailed arrangements – effects which can be obtained almost casually, like a frozen moment in time (*opposite right*).

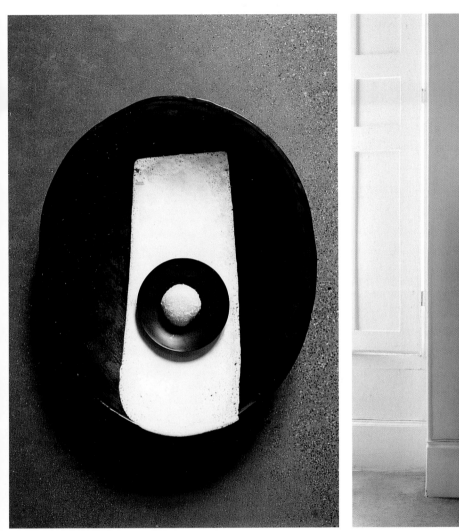

A variety of bathrooms, but all sharing a clean, restrained decorative scheme: in a north Italian farmhouse (*above left*); in an eighteenth-century London townhouse (*above right*); in the Nice house of a noted French product designer (*opposite left*); an essay in elegance in a Sicilian house (*opposite right*).

A pale decoration palette unifies the rooms and interconnecting areas of this Provençal house, making it look deceptively large (*overleaf*). Meticulously detailed points of interest enliven the interior, from plants to pebbles and kindling, with paintings and windows placed in unusual and unexpected positions.

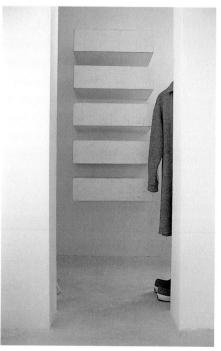

Above the rooftops of Brussels, this loft space (*above left*) enjoys a considerable amount of bright, natural light. Everything in the decorative scheme, from the white painted walls and the sub-dividing hangings to the furniture, is intended to maximize the effect of this luminosity. The old town of Essaouira, on Morocco's Atlantic coast, is a place of fine houses. This example (*above right*), recently restored, is a structure of interlocking terraces and rooms in which the absence of doors and windows, the use of a restrained colour scheme, all contribute to a sensation of movement of light and air from salon to balcony and a paved rooftop garden.

The interiors of this Paris apartment
(*above left*) have been given
a fashionable minimalist treatment,
including a white-painted floor.
Using a similar colour scheme,
but to very different effect, is this
sumptuous interior in Salzburg
(*above right*).

In all the interiors illustrated on these pages the colour white seems to have been used for its own, intrinsic qualities, rather than as mere background decoration. This is especially true of this dining-room in a house in Hammamet (*left above*); in the case of this north Italian farmhouse (*left below*) the colour is used as a unifying device in all the rooms of the building; in a Los Angeles house, painted white throughout, a classic 'Butterfly' chair shows off its sculptural lines (*opposite*).

Monochrome surfaces provide opportunities for the addition of detail to any room setting in witty and inventive ways, often making the best of very personal possessions and tastes. All the 'vignettes' illustrated here (*above* and *opposite*) suggest the intimate involvement of the owners of the houses and apartments in which they occur and sometimes transcend the immediately personal – a collection of shells, for instance, reflects the coastal location of a house in western France.

C H A P T E R 2

BLUE-ISH MOODS
Indigo to Mauves and Violets

Moving on from the neutrality of the monochrome, blue and its related tones are a first step towards using colour to create a 'feel', to influence a mood. In clothing, it flatters, bringing warmer tones in the human face. In decoration, certainly when used with whites or with pale greens, it is also associated with the ocean and the sky, hence its suggestion of things nautical, of life on the shore, where it often appears with an intensity enhanced by the light from the sea. And nowhere does it gleam more brightly, both in interiors and on exterior walls, than in the countries surrounding the Mediterranean.

A blue/grey palette always carries with it resonances of coastal living, where convention sees the colours as those of the water itself beneath an open sky – in this case, photographed near Cape Town (*these pages*).

MAURITIUS

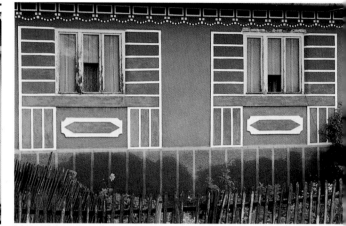

ROMANIA

THAILAND

NORMANDY

COMOROS

CARIBBEAN

The pale blues and greens of outside walls, doors and shutters are improved by a washed and weathered look (*opposite*); their variety is a testimony to the far-ranging quality of Gilles de Chabaneix' photography. The external paint on one of the great palaces of St. Petersburg obviously reflects the extreme weather conditions of the city in a different way (*right*).

Blue and its related hues always carry a certain association with life on the coast; it seems especially appropriate, then, that it is the dominant colour in this house on the Île de Ré, western France (*above*). Another coastal dwelling, typical of the eccentric local domestic architecture, is a house on the island of Chiloë, at the southern tip of Chile (*opposite*).

Blue notes in a variety of very sophisticated, but very different, city dwellings make a positive, dramatic splash of colour: in two Paris apartments (*above left* and *above right*); in a London house (*opposite left*); and in a palatial residence in Istanbul (*opposite right*).

Blues often have the effect of making other colours look more dramatic, either through use as an overall background colour or as a means of emphasizing certain specific features. Against the blue panelling of the dining-room of a Brooklyn apartment, the orange of the illuminated interior of a display cabinet makes a remarkable centrepiece (*left above*). Highlights in an intense blue are a recurring feature in this hotel on the fashionable Caribbean island of Saint-Barthélemy (*left below* and *opposite*); the combination of blue and green reads like a reflection of the lush island vegetation set in a sea of shimmering blues.

Above the bay of San Francisco, the apartment of an eminent fashion designer makes a display of yellow and green highlights on a blue ground (*above left*). A similar play of contrasting colours enlivens the simple lines of this bedroom in a north Italian farmhouse (*above right*). Perforated fabric filters the bright light from the garden of this rustic house near Guatemala City (*opposite left*). In a Rome apartment blue occurs constantly as the colour for storage units (*opposite right*).

The combination of blue and white, both interior and exterior, generally creates a feeling of freshness and brightness, suggesting life by the shore and, indeed, it is a much used decorative device in coastal communities around the world. All the examples illustrated on these pages exude the feeling of the littoral, whether mainland or island: blue wash in an Île de Ré interior (*above left*); on the terrace of a Miami hotel (*above right*); a veranda in the Bahamas (*opposite left*); shutters in Tangier (*opposite right*).

Blue combined with white is omnipresent on the Greek islands; significantly, both colours are those of the Greek national flag. In this house (*left*) in Lindos, on the island of Rhodes, blue is used as a counterpoint device to contrast with the overall white of the walls, most spectacularly as the dominant colour of the floor.

On Cycladic Santorini blue occurs everywhere, outside and inside, outlining doors and windows, applied to tables, cupboards and chairs, and generally making a colourful effect against the white pozzuolana of the houses (*above right*).

This house on Salina, in the Aeolian Islands, also has the blue/white decorative scheme so typical of cool, summery rooms (*below right*).

The blues are a varied and versatile family, capable of producing very different effects. Informal washes create a pleasant lived-in feeling in a Moroccan house (*above left*). A more formal effect is achieved in this bedroom of an Umbrian house by painting the walls in a uniform colour (*above right*). Whimsy and fantasy are the keynotes of this Paris apartment (*opposite left*), where the dominant colours are blue, mauve and pink – a very different effect to the feeling of calm luxury in another Paris apartment (*opposite right*).

A pale blue wash, varying in intensity, links the rooms of the Corsican house of an eminent publicist. Fresh and somehow cooling in its effect, this use of colour is the very essence of Mediterranean style (*left* and *opposite*).

Blue washes are put to slightly comic effect in this chair 'installation' in the studio of a Parisian painter (*overleaf*).

The paler blues bring a generally peaceful, soothing feeling to the spaces in which they are applied, from the casual to the formal, or even the utilitarian: a terrace in Morocco (*above left*); a bedroom in a Corsican house (*above right*); an elegant Paris apartment (*opposite left*); a textile designer's Paris kitchen (*opposite right*).

Soft, greyish blues link the many oddly shaped spaces in this converted cheese factory in Milan (*left* and *opposite*). Against this background – which includes a floor of Moroccan tiles – the owner has created several points of visual interest by the display of dramatically shaped objects and furniture. The colour, combined with reflected light and the lighting, creates a subtle glow through the main room. Corridors, stairwells and connecting areas in the conversion are used as display areas for paintings and objects.

Pale blues pick out the storage units
in this Paris apartment owned by
a distinguished fabric designer (*left*).

Blues, almost shading to green, are used to lighten the hallways and staircase of this elegant Versailles house, the home of an artist-designer (*right*).

Pale blue shelving forms an almost sculptural element in this Paris apartment (*above*), providing infinite possibilities for the display of interesting objects. Two metal support pillars have been inserted to open up the sitting-room and the dining area, thus allowing the shelf unit to make a greater impact, along with the immense 'Trapèze' table and the 'Standard' chairs, designed by Jean Prouvé.

Another example of open storage
elements enlivening a dining area:
this striking blue dresser in a Sicilian
kitchen immediately extends the
room's decorative possibilities (*above*).

Bedroom blues again (*left* and *opposite*): various shades, from the walls to the storage units, dominate this interior treatment in an Île de Ré house. The colour plays a more subtle role in the bedroom of a modernist Los Angeles dwelling in the form of a simple art-installation panel that can be repositioned or, indeed, recoloured.

The paler shades of blue, turquoise, and blues-going-on-green provide subtle colouring in sometimes unexpected places (*left* and *opposite*), from chestnut furniture in a Provençal house to the livery of a nineteen-fifties Plymouth automobile in Havana.

Overleaf
An extraordinary private collection of maiolica bowls and vases shows off the startling effect of the greenish blue hues.

PARIS

PARIS

MADEIRA

PARIS

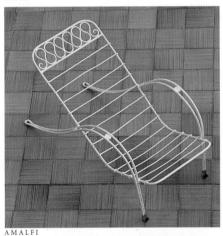

AMALFI

PARIS

HELSINKI

HAVANA

QUEBEC

In a rambling nineteenth-century French house, designer Philippe Renaud has created what are, effectively, a series of 'cabinets of curiosities' – rooms of carefully assembled clutter and disparate objects (*above left* and *right, opposite left*): eclectic wall displays spread on to a screen; a painted plaster head, stuffed birds are stacked against a painting, all perched on a Louis Seize chair. But, as a unifying background to the many different compositions in the house, the designer has chosen a palette of pale blue-greens. A more orderly display is that of the owner's collection of earthenware in this San Francisco apartment against a colour more distinctly tending towards the green (*opposite right*).

Streamlined forms and cool greens and blues dominate the interlocking spaces of this modernist house in Los Angeles (*above left* and *right*, and *opposite*). The overall effect is to soften the utilitarian aspect of the fittings; interestingly, too, the summery interior colours seem to reflect that of the swimming-pool outside.

Greens and a pale blue wash on the walls create a distinctly rustic, homely atmosphere in this Provence house (*above*). In another rural French house – in the countryside but close to Paris – the owner has used a pale blue wash on the upper part of the walls of the connecting spaces, while picking out the storage element on the landings in a deeper blue (*opposite*).

CHAPTER 3

RICH REDS AND PALE PINKS

Colours of Luxury

Reds are aggressive and assertive, although their softer side is apparent in the pastel pinks of the latter pages of this chapter. This is a family of colours which can often suggest great opulence and a sense of luxury when used in all-over treatments, especially when extended to fabrics and upholstery. These colours can also shock and surprise when creating points of focus and interest in otherwise monochromatic environments. A red chair or rug can transform blandness into visual excitement, while pinks of varying shades and intensity convey a sense of equanimity and well-being as well as fun. And, finally, to the browns: here, the colours of panelling and wooden frames encourage feelings of strength and security.

Rich reds flourish in nature: sorting the chilli harvest in Rajasthan (*opposite*); the deep reds of Provençal cherries (*this page*).

Within the cool, modern scheme of a country house near Bologna, the owners have introduced a numbe of highlights of dramatic, rich colour (*left* and *opposite*). Often these are in the form of important individual items of furniture that can be moved about or even replaced, such as upholstered chairs and wall display units.

Supremely functional, but with quirky decorative structures, often drawing upon a palette of reds, this sitting-cum-dining-cum-kitchen area fits neatly into a converted roof cavity in Paris (*above left* and *right*, and *opposite*). The demands on space of modern urban living are nowhere better illustrated than in this series of related spaces, enlivened with such elements as red perspex screens, red flashes on the blinds, and a magnificent array of red sofas.

Strong, earthy colours are the very stuff of Provence (*opposite*), to be found in textiles, crockery and, here, on the walls of a traditional house (*opposite*). The fire-engine red of this dining-room makes a marvellous background for a Cézanne-like still-life on the table, reflecting the intensity of the wall and floor colours. In other instances, reds form a special feature within a decorative scheme: one of Philippe Renaud's 'arrangements' (*far left above*); in a terrace in 'Chinoiserie' style (*left above*); in a wooden châlet near Grenoble (*far left below*); and in a Paris apartment where splashes of colour are thrown into sharp relief against a plain wood floor (*left below*).

Rich Oriental reds are the theme of these four interiors; in some cultures it is the colour of happiness, but in these rooms it is certainly the colour of luxury: an intimate part of an Istanbul residence (*above left*); the dominant colour in this 'chinoiserie' – themed tea room (*above right*); the rich patina of an antique Chinese cupboard in a Versailles house (*opposite left*); and an overall treatment in a Paris apartment, reflecting some of the tones in the flat-weave rugs and cushions (*opposite right*).

This bedroom (*above*), a play of reds, pinks and golds, is the design of an eminent Parisian creator of women's clothing from the finest fabrics. Although deep, rich colours are not those most immediately associated with the intimacy of the bedroom, there is a warm, inviting quality about this arrangement, enhanced by the glowing, soft forms of the hangings.

The interiors of the Provence house
of a Parisian florist-designer pick
up on the traditional colours of
the region (*above*). In the study,
the warm terracotta of the painted
walls finds partial echoes in
the floral arrangement and the
long *banquette*.

Reds can certainly bring rooms to life, especially when used in unlikely ways in unlikely places – floors and doors for instance, rather than walls. The Paris home of a ceramic artist has painted doors for dramatic impact in an allover pale scheme (*above left*). Another Paris apartment, belonging to a designer of amusing, quirky objects and lighting , sets off white walls with stained floors (*above right*). The relatively spartan, monochrome interiors of this north Italian house make ideal settings for brilliantly coloured rugs and large works of art (*opposite left*). A painted floor covering provides the finishing touch to a small guest bedroom in the Paris apartment of a fabric designer (*opposite right*).

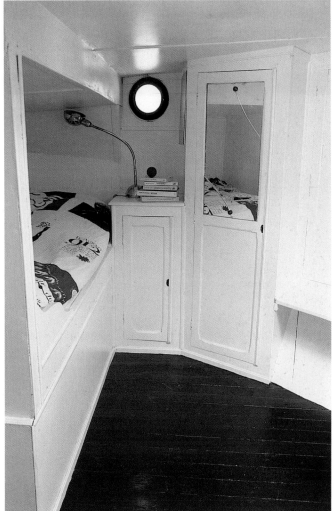

In this Paris apartment (*left above* and *left below*, and *opposite*) rich reds have again been used as a counterpoint to the overall sobriety of layout and of the design and colours of the furniture. Here, a wall has been picked out for contrasting treatment; there, a sumptuously coloured carpet provides an opulent setting for the restrained monochromes of the furniture.

These contemporary interpretations of the Empire style (*left above*, *opposite* and *overleaf*) are the work of a Parisian furniture designer whose creations are characterized by a signature 'rope' effect on their structural parts. The impression of stylish luxury conveyed by their traditional forms and exquisite craftsmanship is much reinforced by the rich red of their upholstery. Similarly, the soft furnishings of this Paris apartment – upholstery and curtains – constitute focal points of richness and opulence in an otherwise restrained setting (*left below*).

Red, in various strengths and shades is without doubt the colour of visual drama. A row of Le Corbusier's classic 'Grand Confort' armchairs, unusually upholstered in red leather rather than black, make an impressive display in the studio of a leading Paris fashion designer (*left above*). And – more literally dramatic – reds are the dominant colours in this film set for the movie *Tanguy* (*left below*). The sheer flamboyance of the colour finds marvellous expression in the dresses and veils of two Rajasthani temple dancers (*opposite*).

Whimsical red and deep pinks showcase the designs of a Paris studio (*opposite*). A more trenchant statement of the dramatic strength of red are the chairs in the cool, monochrome interiors of this north Italian house (*right*).

In matters of colour, art – or at least decorative art – often imitates nature (*overleaf*): in a restored Federal house in New York state.

In the pages which follow (*to p.143*) the surprising effects of a range of reds, pinks and purples is demonstrated in this Paris apartment – a combination of modernism and anti-modernism in about equal amounts. In the bathroom and related dressing areas, deep pinks and near-purples combine dramatically with pale blues (*these pages*).

Classic chairs by Jacobsen and
Eames fly the colours of modernism
in what is otherwise an anti-
modernist statement of exaggerated
forms, colours and visual jokes,
including Kermit the Frog (*left* and
above). The whimsy of the pinks
and blues is repeated in the kitchen
area (*overleaf*), and again tempered
by the black and white floor and the
Jacobsen dining chairs.

The apartment (*opposite* and *right*) is full of shocks and surprises, most of them perpetrated in an assortment of bold, assertive colours. Furniture, lighting and the whole decoration scheme combine to produce a remarkably invigorating effect.

There is almost a behind-the-scenes look about this room setting (*left*) in the Villa Medici, Rome. Such scenes, rather than the great public rooms, can prove especially inspirational for contemporary interior designers. In contrast, this London apartment (*opposite*) is already elaborately designed and detailed to accommodate the owner's collection of 'chinoiserie'.

Pinks in varied contexts: another corner in the apartment illustrated on *pp. 136–143* (*above left*); glazes on a range of the delicate bowls created by Christiane Perrochon, a ceramic artist who works in Tuscany (*above right*); a floral balcony in Provence (*opposite left*); an amusingly seated Ernest Race chair originally designed for the 1951 Festival of Britain (*opposite right*).

Material wealth in rich reds and pinks: a textile worker in Rajasthan (*opposite*); the flowing robes of a Rajasthani woman (*above left*); deep upholstery in a Tuileries apartment, Paris (*above right*); similar tones in a New York interior are echoed on exterior shutters in the same city (*overleaf*).

Dark reddish browns often carry
with them implications of comfort,
of luxury, even when used in a
minimalist décor, as in this Los
Angeles house (*above right*). In more
conventional settings (*above left*,
opposite left and *right*), the effect is
undoubtedly warm and welcoming.

A homely red-brown is the
dominant colour in this recreation
of an eighteenth-century New
England kitchen (*above*).

Brown highlights in the form of picture frames, cushions and bed linen add luxurious grace notes to this room in a low impact hotel in the Australian outback (*above*).

Strange red-brown markings decorate
the votive stones of this crude shrine
in Hampi, Karnataka, India (*above*),
an apparently casual but inspirational
colour combination.

The upper gallery of one of the fine old houses of Essaouira leads to the bedrooms (*above*). The all-white treatment, which extends throughout the structure's interlocking terraces and rooms, is broken by the graphic outlines of the brown-stained door and window frames (*above*).

CHAPTER 4

SUNLIT CITRUS

Lemon, Lime and the Alfresco Look

Yellows and greens immediately evoke the outside – the colours of sunlit gardens, of growth and plenty. These are colours to illuminate interiors, suggesting the freshness of the world outside applied to the comforts and facilities of the world inside. The shades and applications vary enormously. Vibrant yellows, for instance, can be used to highlight furniture, as in the Frida Kahlo house, or to emphasize single features in an off-white interior; they can also be used for overall treatments, as with the earthy, ochrous pigments of Provence. Paler hues provide ideal backgrounds for the display of works of art or ceramics; they can also lend an air of quiet distinction to any interior.

Yellows and greens are the colours which most potently express the bounty of nature, and most emphatically a sunlit nature: the sunny side of a street in Saigon (*opposite*); members of the squash family in a Provençal market (*this page*).

Nothing enlivens an interior as much as the introduction into it of fresh, natural produce in the form of flowers and fruit (*right* and *opposite*). Similar effects of freshness and light are achieved by the display of objects reflecting the garden palettes of yellows and greens. Jacobsen chairs in these colours bring an alfresco feeling to the dining area of a northern Italian house, otherwise notable for the reticence of its overall decorative scheme (*overleaf*).

The choice of materials and colours for this veranda of a Saigon house (*opposite*) emphasizes the role of such a space as a bridge between the exterior and interior, a place leading inwards yet still open to the surrounding vegetation. In this northern Italian house, the outside has been brought inside in the form of a green, garden-style chair (*right*).

This remarkable display of furniture
highlighted in an acid yellow is in
the former home of the artist Frida
Kahlo in Mexico City (*left*).
The colour does indeed stand out
when used on a single, dominant
interior feature, as in this
Los Angeles house (*above*).

These yellows, of varying shades and intensity, all contrive to create a joyful, luminous atmosphere in very varied environments. The owner of an Irish country house has chosen it as the background against which to display a collection of blue-and-white china (*above left*). Yellow is used on ceilings, walls and floors in this house on the Île de Ré (*above right*); the latter are rendered even more intriguing by the incorporation of locally found pebbles to form complex patterns in them. A deep yellow casts a warm glow in a sunlit Paris kitchen (*opposite left*). There is a pleasantly country air about the yellows and greens used in this rural retreat at Bois Colombe, near Paris (*opposite right* and *overleaf*).

A subdued, ochrous yellow subtly
reflects the sunlight falling through
the window of a bedroom of a
traditional Moroccan house in
Marrakesh (*above*).

A similarly subdued but earthy
yellow provides a warm background
to a veritable feast laid out on the
rustic table of a house in Saint-
Rémy-de-Provence (*above*).

These vibrant yellows (*above* and *opposite*) in the kitchen of a house in a small village near Les Baux are the very stuff of Provence, to be found in textiles, crockery and, here, on the walls of a traditional dwelling.

Warm-toned yellows, especially, are associated with the crockery of the region; how appropriate, then, that the walls of the simple kitchen-dining area of the house should be painted in those tones.

As a means of creating pleasant domestic environments, the combination of colour and the display of interesting objects need not be confined to the principal living areas of the home. Kitchens, especially, have their claim to this aspect of the home-maker's art, because they are usually so full of intriguing shapes and forms, looking all the better against sensitively applied colour: a house in Uzès, Provence (*above*); a painter's apartment in Paris (*opposite*).

Yellow used as positive colour, either in detail or in allover schemes, brings a warm glow to big-city environments: in the apartment of a Paris fashion designer (*above left*); detail in a white-painted New York bathroom (*above right*); strong colour in a corner of a Los Angeles house (*opposite left*); and even stronger, more assertive application, reflecting the furniture, in a house in Buenos Aires (*opposite right*).

The pale yellows of the walls of this
Corsican house (*above* and *opposite*)
show the versatility of the colour in
its various tones. It can be dominant,
both on large areas or on small details,
but it can also be gently toned down to
background status like a buttermilk
wash, as here.

As a means of introducing a bright, sunny tone to any part of a home, the colour yellow has few competitors, with its resonances of the brighter side of an outdoor life. Typically, it is a colour much used in the furniture, textiles and ceramics of Provence (*above left*). In a Paris apartment, it showcases elements of whimsy on a bedroom chest of drawers (*above right*). As a background, it is neither too laid-back nor too assertive: panelling behind a highly sculptural lamp in an Île-de-Ré house (*opposite left*); a brilliant setting for a collection of blue-and-white ceramics in an Irish country house (*opposite right*).

Yellow upholstery provides point
of focus in the ground floor of a
modernist house in Los Angeles
(*left*), reflecting the light which fl
in from the surrounding terraces
gardens. This view is from one of
loft floors, walled by glass, which
cantilevered out over the main sit
area. Similar shades of yellow are
used to create a couple of brillian
spots in the garden of a northern
Italian house (*opposite*).

The work of designer Philippe
Renaud is characterized by
arrangements of *outré* objects rather
than by elaborate decorative work.
In this bedroom (*above*), however, in
a rambling French country house, he
has used a handsome, yellow-striped
Laura Ashley wallpaper.

Yellow, especially in pale tones, is remarkable for its versatility, equally at home in the bedroom of a city apartment (*above left*), or in the kitchen of a country house in Corsica (*above right*).

The rooms in a Marrakesh house
(*above left* and *above right*),
including the bathroom, are treated
in a greenish-yellow wash. This
contrasts with the structural features
left exposed as rose-coloured
brickwork to outline certain features
or even whole walls. Antique hanging
lamps and terracotta pots form other
decorative elements.

Two more examples of the unobtrusive versatility of the yellows in bathrooms; this application (*above left*) is in a Corsican country house; in an eco-friendly Californian house the colour combines with the blue-green of the floor (*above right*).

A pale, discreet yellow runs
as a unifying theme throughout
the interconnecting spaces of
a modernist Los Angeles home
(*opposite* and *above left*). But look
how vibrant the bright yellow
of the beaker on the table seems.
In the apartment of a Parisian fabric
designer (*above right*), the pale
yellow of the walls provides an
unassuming background to works
of art and furniture.

A return to the greens: the soft
colours of celadon ware seem
uniquely appropriate to the taking
of tea in a Saigon house (*opposite*);
a variety of greens add grace notes
of elegance to the apartment of
a Parisian artist (*above*).

CHAPTER 5

NATURALS AND NEUTRALS

Beige, Cream and Earth Colours

The subjects of this section of the book are those parts of the decorator's palette which do not fit easily into the four-colour families of black, cyan, magenta and yellow. In many of the examples illustrated, the colours and the materials to which they are applied seem closely related: rich browns of wooden panelling; ochrous terracotta on the interior and exterior walls of rustic houses; pale washes that seem to be the original colour of the plaster beneath. But however restrained, all these decorative schemes are just as effective in their own way as the more assertive colour treatments illustrated in preceding chapters.

Earthy colours and rough textures characterize the oldest houses in the city of Zihuatanejo on the Pacific coast of Mexico (*these pages*).

MOROCCO

PROVENCE

NAPLES

BARCELONA

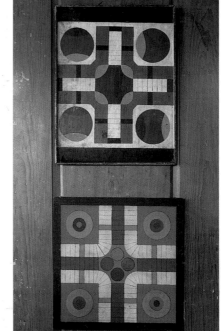

ÎLE DE RÉ

BALI

These are the colours of natural
materials (*opposite* and *right*),
of stone, wood, clay or even dried
leaves. They may also provide the
inspiration for an extension to the
decorator's palette for those browns,
beiges and creams which so often
play second fiddle to the more
assertive colour ranges treated
in foregoing sections of this book.
Yet, often in combination with
rich pattern and texture, they have
a timeless decorative vitality all
their own.

The traditional dwellings of San Cristobal de las Casas, in the central highlands of Mexico, have a sun-baked aspect which is often reflected in the various shades of terracotta applied to their exteriors (*above left*). A similarly earthy effect, in many senses, is amply expressed in this glimpse of life in Luxor, Egypt (*above right*).

Mediterranean warmth finds its
architectural expression in the
terracotta façades of the palatial
buildings of Rome and in the cities
of Tuscany (*above left* and *right*).

Local architecture, local forms, local
materials, local colour – all these
examples somehow combine these
elements in a particularly intimate
and convincing way: a street in
Marrakesh (*above left*); two interiors
in a house in the same city (*above
right* and *opposite left*); a maze of
spaces in a house in Guatemala City
(*opposite right*).

The reds and russets of the houses of Roussillon, a hill village between the mountains of the Vaucluse and the Lubéron in Provence, are literally the colours of the local earth (*left*). Many of the dwellings are made of locally quarried stone and decorated with locally produced tiles, all tinted by the powder from the amazing ochre cliffs on which the village stands and from which a range of earth-coloured paints have been derived. This kitchen setting is in the home of a distinguished chef and author of cookery books.

Beiges, terracotta, rich reds and an extraordinary collection of hanging lamps all combine to produce an interior of great opulence in an Istanbul house (*right*).

Ochres and marbled effects are used to delineate features in this traditional Moroccan house (*opposite*), to add a distinctly warm glow to a Provençal bathroom (*right above*), to produce a distinctly sybaritic look in the bathroom of a north Italian villa (*right below*).

The 'natural' colour schemes of these
two rooms – one in Marrakesh
(*above left*) and the other in
Roussillon (*above right*) both reflect
and contrast with the variety of
colour in the flat-weave rugs.
In the kitchen of the Marrakesh
house a terracotta wash defines
the food preparation area (*opposite*).

The presence of Roussillon's famous red ochre is only too evident in the walls of this kitchen / dining-room (*above left*); the faded yellows of the pottery on the side table complete a display of typical Provençal tones.

These rich and subtle colours are used in the more sophisticated decorative schemes of two Paris apartments (*above right* and *opposite left*, and *opposite right*).

Strong, earthy colours are the very essence of Provence, to be found in local pottery and in the interiors of even the most modest of traditional houses (*left above* and *opposite above*). Locally produced fabrics, too, are often characterized by similar russet and ochre tints.

The subtle interplay of outside light and the rich, deep colours of the interior is fundamental to the charms of the traditional Moroccan house (*left below*). The room itself is simply furnished, but the sumptuous colours of rugs and walls bespeak luxury.

A beige / yellow background helps to suffuse this highly individual Paris apartment with a warm light (*right below*). Faded reds and beiges complement each other in the fabrics and flat-weave rugs.

In their very different ways – in Paris (*above left*), Marrakesh (*above right*), Corsica (*opposite left*), and Provence (*opposite right*) – all the rooms illustrated here demonstrate one design characteristic: that they are intended to be places of comfort and that this effect is achieved by very personal attention to choice of colour and content.

Overleaf
The brown and reddish hues of this Los Angeles interior were partly inspired by the colours of the surrounding countryside and are a continuation of the tones of a sculptural composition around the pool outside. The room, with its ceiling-level, clerestory-style windows for light and air, is composed of blocks of colour like elements in a desert landscape.

PROVENCE

SYDNEY

MAURITIUS

PROVENCE

HELSINKI

PROVENCE

All the examples of colour illustrated here seem to draw much of their significance from the materials to which they are applied or from which they derive – reddish plasterwork and wrought iron, the patina of polished wood or the glow of old panelling, as in the apartment of a Parisian designer-decorator (*right*), or the yellowish tones of rough-hewn stone.

Subdued browns and beiges extend throughout this Los Angeles house (*far left above* and *below*). The colours pick up those of the rocks and soil of the surrounding garden, which also contains a collection of abstract sculpture coloured in similar tones. The walls of this Paris apartment repeat some of the light browns in the complex wood-inlay floor (*left above*). Eighteenth-century browns pick out the wooden feature in a house in a conservation village in Massachusetts (*left below*).

Rusty pinks highlight the major features in two very different environments: a palace in Delhi (*right above*); a rural house in Provence, preserved as a folk museum (*right below*).

Staircases, passages and corridors are the spaces of transition within the home, and thus of great importance. Yet their frequently awkward shapes and comparative lack of windows do make them a challenge for the decorator. Here, in a preserved French country house (*these pages*) a pale pinkish-brown picks out the wooden features, leaving walls and ceiling a neutral off-white to maximize the effect of any available light.

The beauty of browns: a transitional
space in a traditional Moroccan
house provides relief from the sunlit
courtyard (*far left above*); in
another Moroccan house the effects
of sunlight in the courtyard
are mitigated by the application
of a light-brown wash (*left above*);
browns can also evoke a sense
of luxury, as in these two Paris
apartments (*far left* and *left below*).
The door surrounds and exterior
walls of this Rajasthan house
make decorative play with a whole
variety of browns (*opposite*).

Overleaf
A Normandy interior (*left*) is
rendered warm and comfortable
by the rich browns of the wooden
panelling and the distribution
around the house of highly personal
objects and belongings. A more
urbane use of a similar colour range
occurs in this Paris apartment
(*right*), where the owners have
sought to create an overall harmony
in the arrangement of furnishings,
objects and paintings in keeping
with the general Empire-style look
of the space.

Browns and beiges in the dining-room; there is something to be said here that colour should not distract from the food and the joys of eating: in a restored château in the Lubéron, Provence (*above left*); in a London townhouse (*above right*); in two settings from the same house in Istanbul (*opposite left* and *right*).

Simple colours as befitting simple
Mediterranean bathrooms: two
traditional versions in Morocco
(*above left* and *right*); in Provence,
with the characteristic large tiles of
the region (*opposite left*); a modern
variation on a Moroccan bathroom
(*opposite right*).

Colours of cinnamon, mustard
and sand link the interlocking
interior spaces of this apartment
near Paris (*left* and *above*).
The colour scheme is carried
through to the flooring, furniture
and every aspect of the room.

These two kitchens have all the classic qualities of traditional French country décor (*above* and *opposite*): simple but stylish rustic furniture, neutral colours relieved by decorative tiling, open shelves, bare floors, utilitarian light fittings and matt finishes.

More examples of the French country kitchen; as befitting a culture so devoted to the culinary arts, these rooms clearly play an important role in their respective houses, one in Provence (*above*) and one near Paris (*opposite*). Against the neutral backgrounds, attention is focused on the wealth of equipment, of crockery and other artefacts arranged on shelves and working surfaces.

Mustard yellows of very different shades and intensities put to use in a variety of environments: highlighting recesses in a Paris apartment notable for its understated modernism (*above left*); as background to the owner's collection of art in a Brussels house (*above right* and *opposite right*); a very different, certainly more rustic yellow is used as a wash on some of the internal walls of a French country house (*opposite left*).

BOMBAY

BANGKOK

PARIS

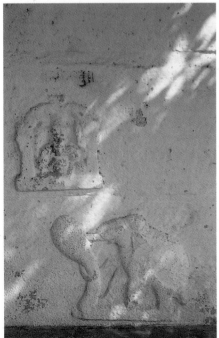

HAMPI

NEPAL

CAPE TOWN

Light colours in decoration and furniture set the tone of this Île de Ré house (*right*) – one somehow appropriate to a situation enjoying the brilliant light from the sea. And everywhere in the world, subtle, reticent colouring is present, wherever we care to look for it (*opposite*).

Natural tones in very different
rooms: in a Marrakesh kitchen
(*above left*); combining to create
a quietly sumptuous bedroom
in a house in western France (*above
right*); classical simplicity in a Paris
apartment (*opposite left*); warmer
colours to soften the outside light in
the interior of a traditional Moroccan
courtyard house (*opposite right*).

In the light of Provence and a generally benevolent climate, which encourages the spending of time outside, interior decoration often seems most effective when it sticks to simple forms and simple colours, as in this house in Saint-Rémy-de-Provence (*above*). And although the form of the bed in this Nice house (*opposite*) is elaborate enough, a similar simplicity is the keynote of the decoration.

Four interiors where colour or even lack of it seems peculiarly expressive of the materials and surfaces of the walls: a panelled house in Normandy (*above left*); untreated rendering on the substantial walls of two Provençal kitchens (*above right* and *opposite left*); smooth yellows in a London townhouse (*opposite right*).

A distinguished French decorator's preferred approach to interior desig_ is well illustrated in this landing in a French country house (*opposite*). The colours and materials of the walls are left to express themselves, leaving attention focused on the quirky, surreal arrangements of objects. Less eccentric, but equall_ reticent in terms of background are these two seating arrangements: in a rural Australian hotel (*left above*); in a traditional Moroccan house (*left below*).

Overleaf
All these seven interiors have a quietly understated feel about them – places where objects and furniture can come into their own without being overwhelmed by the aggressive use of colour and décor.

PARIS

PROVENCE

PARIS

NORMANDY

MOROCCO

PARIS

An eclectic mix of furniture is one notable aspect of this very restrained Paris apartment (*left above*). Indeed, some articles look as though they could just as easily figure on terrace or balcony. A similar restraint characterizes this elegant setting in a country house near Paris (*left below*).

Contrasting styles in Paris
apartments: one is coolly
conventional, with traditional
furniture and fittings (*right above*);
the other – an attic space – has all
the quirkiness of Philippe Renaud's
decorative style, in which odd-
looking furniture and 'fun' objects
can combine together against
a relatively neutral background
(*right below*). Both rely heavily
for effect on the restrained use
of natural colours.

Four vignettes: all these
arrangements of small objects
draw on a palette of 'earth' colours,
both for the objects themselves
and the surrounding décor.

Page numbers in *italic* refer to illustrations

A

Aeolian Islands *83*
Amalfi *101*
Art Deco 12
Art Nouveau 12
Australia *16, 155, 246*
Auvergne *30*

B

Bahamas *81*
balconies *62, 147*; *see also* terraces; verandas
Bali *40, 196*
Bangkok *238*
Barcelona *196*
bathrooms *40–41, 58–59, 136, 152, 153, 178, 188, 189, 205, 228–29*
bedrooms *38, 43, 51, 72, 78, 83, 84, 87, 90, 91, 98, 99, 118, 119, 120, 123, 172, 186, 187, 211, 212, 240, 242–43*
blinds *114*
blues *68–109*
Bois Colombe *169, 170–71*
Bologna *32, 112, 113*
Bombay *238*
bowls: Christiane Perrochon *146*
Brussels *29, 30, 32, 33, 44, 62, 236, 237*
Buenos Aires *179*

C

California *189*
Canada *24*
Cape Town *68–69, 238*
Caribbean *70*
ceramics *182, 183*
chairs *17, 35, 39, 42, 46, 47, 52–53, 55, 62, 64, 72, 74, 76, 77, 79, 80, 84, 85, 88–89, 90, 94, 95, 97, 100, 101, 104, 105, 106, 107, 108, 112, 113, 114, 117, 118, 119, 125, 132, 133, 138, 139, 142, 145, 147, 150, 154, 155, 162–63, 165, 169, 170–71, 174, 175, 176, 180–181, 184, 187, 188, 191, 201, 203,* *204, 206, 208, 214, 222, 224, 225–29, 231, 235, 236, 237, 244, 245, 250, 251*; 'Butterfly' *65*; Eames *138–39*; garden-style *165*; 'Grand Confort' *130*; Jacobsen *138–39, 140–41, 162–63*; Louis Seize *105*; 'Standard' *96*
Chile *73*
Chiloë *26, 73*
china *see* crockery
chinoiserie *35, 116, 118, 145*
citrus colours *158–93*
collections *66–67*; earthenware *105*; maiolica *102–3*; shells *67*
Comoros *70*
corridors *92, 93, 220*
Corsica *28, 38, 40, 42, 86–87, 90, 180–81, 187, 189, 213*
crockery *117, 168, 174, 175, 192, 210, 235*
curtains *126, 128–29*
cushions *119, 155*

D

Delhi *219*
dining-rooms/dining areas *42, 64, 76, 108, 117, 161, 166, 174, 226–27*
Directoire furniture *54–55*
doors *26, 27, 29, 31, 70–71, 122, 157*
dressers *97*
Dubuffet, Jean *54–55*

E

Earth colours *see* naturals and neutrals
earthenware *105*
Egypt *198*
Empire style *225*; contemporary interpretations of *126–29*
Essaouira *62, 157*

F

Fabrics *210, 211*; *see also* textiles
façades *14–15, 28, 199*
fireplaces *44–45, 204, 222, 250, 251*
floors *122, 123*; painted *63, 122*; tiled *92, 93*; wood *116*

flowers *134, 135, 160*
France *39, 67, 72, 109, 220–21, 232, 234, 237, 240, 247*
fruit *160*

G

Galleries *157*
gardens *185*; rooftop *62*
Granada *16*
Greece *30*
Grenoble *116*
Guatemala City *79, 201*

H

Hallways *95*
Hammamet *64*
Hampi *156, 238*
Havana *101*
Helsinki *101, 216*

I

Île de Ré *41, 72, 80, 98, 168, 182, 196, 238*
India *156*
Ireland *168, 183*
Istanbul *28, 30, 75, 118, 203, 227*
Italy *58, 64, 78, 123, 133, 162–63, 166, 185, 20.*

K

Kahlo, Frida *159, 166–67*
Karnataka *156*
kitchens *51, 91, 97, 106, 140–41, 154, 169, 173–77, 187, 202, 206, 219, 232–33, 234–35, 240, 245*

L

Lamps *36, 50, 74, 77, 78, 85, 86, 98, 99, 116, 121, 124, 170–71, 180, 181, 182, 188, 201, 203, 226, 236, 237, 239, 244, 251, 252–53*
Laura Ashley *186*
Le Corbusier *130*
Les Baux *174*
Lindos *82*
London *45, 47, 58, 75, 145, 227, 245*
Los Angeles *45, 65, 99, 106–7, 152, 167, 179, 184, 190–91, 214–15, 218*

Lubéron 202, *226*
Luxor *198*

Madeira *101*
Madrid *26*
maiolica *102–3*
Marrakesh *17, 20, 31, 34, 172, 188, 200, 201, 206, 207, 212, 240*
Massachusetts *218*
Mauritius *6, 70, 216*
Mediterranean *13, 69*
Mexico *194–95, 198*
Mexico City *166–67*
Miami *80*
Michoacan *9*
Milan *92, 93*
minimalism *63, 152*
Miró, Joan *54–55*
modernism *184, 190–91, 236*
monochrome *12–13, 14–15, 24, 25, 26–67*
Morelia *9*
Morocco *41, 84, 92, 93, 172, 196, 204, 210, 222, 228, 229, 241, 246, 248*
Mykonos *33*

Naples *196*
naturals and neutrals *194–253*
Nepal *26, 238*
New England *154*
New York (city) *46, 150–51, 178*
New York (state) *14, 27*
Nice *59, 243*
Normandy *70, 224, 244, 248*

Panelling *217, 244*
Paris *16, 35, 43, 44, 52–56, 57, 63, 74, 85, 88–89, 91, 94, 96, 101, 114–15, 116, 119, 122, 123, 124–125, 126–29, 132, 136–43, 146, 149, 169, 177, 178, 182, 191, 193, 209, 211, 212, 218, 222, 224, 230–31, 235, 236, 238, 241, 248, 250, 251*

Perrochon, Christiane *146*
pinks *111–57*
pottery *208.*
pozzuolana *83*
Prouvé, Jean *96*
Provence *7, 60–61, 100, 108, 111, 117, 121, 147, 159, 176, 182, 196, 202, 210, 213, 216, 219, 226, 229, 234, 244, 245, 248*

Quebec *24, 101*

Rajasthan *110, 148, 223*
reds *111–57*
Renaud, Philippe *104, 116, 186, 251*
Rhodes *26, 82*
Romania *70*
Rome *79, 199;* Villa Medici *144*
Roussillon *202, 205, 206, 208*
rugs *119, 123, 124, 170–71, 210, 211, 250*

Saigon *158, 164, 192*
Saint-Barthélemy *76, 77*
St. Petersburg *71*
Saint-Rémy-de-Provence *173, 242*
Salina *83*
Salzburg *63*
San Cristobal de las Casas *11, 198*
San Francisco *15, 78, 105, 146;* 'painted ladies' *10*
Santorini *83*
screens *114*
shells *67*
shelving *54, 96, 153, 166, 167, 235*
showers *see* bathrooms
shutters *70, 151*
Sicily *48–51, 59, 97*
Slovakia *15, 16*
sofas *35, 37, 48–49, 50, 54, 64, 77, 91, 93, 114, 115, 125–29, 130, 132, 133, 135, 138–39, 144, 155, 170–71, 181, 184, 190, 193, 215, 225, 230–31, 239, 241, 246, 250*

Sri Lanka *22–23, 30*
stairs *32–33, 86, 92, 95, 169, 170, 220*
statuary *29, 56, 168*
Stockholm *30*
storage *97, 109*
studies *121*
Sydney *216*

Tables *39, 42, 54, 55, 61, 62, 64, 78, 100, 106, 107, 114, 115, 125, 135, 169, 173–76, 179, 187, 191, 201, 204, 206, 213, 226, 227, 231–34, 239, 244, 245, 250, 251;* dining *36, 76, 108, 117, 140, 162–63, 167–68, 213;* 'Trapèze' *96*
Tangier *81*
terraces *90, 147; see also* balconies; verandas
terracotta *188, 199*
textiles *117, 174*
Thailand *70*
tiles *202, 232; see also* floors, tiled
transitional spaces *32–33*
Tuscany *146*

Umbria *29, 84*
upholstery *126–29*
Uzès *176*

Vaucluse *202*
verandas *164; see also* balconies; terraces
Versailles *36–37, 95, 119*

Walls *125, 173, 210, 237, 245;* glass *184;* outside *70;* painted *121;* wall displays *104, 112*
window frames/surrounds *26, 157*
wood *38, 217*

Zihuatanejo *194–95*

ACKNOWLEDGMENTS

Cover images © Estate of Gilles de Chabaneix

Designed by Stafford Cliff
Index compiled by Anna Bennett

First published in the United Kingdom in 2008 by
Thames & Hudson Ltd
181A High Holborn
London WC1V 7QX

First paperback edition 2014

The Way We Live: With Colour
© 2008 Thames & Hudson Ltd, London

All photographs
© 2008 Estate of Gilles de Chabaneix

Design and layout
© 2008 Stafford Cliff

Text and captions
© 2008 Thames & Hudson Ltd, London

British Library Cataloguing-in-Publication Data
A catalogue record for this book is available from
the British Library

ISBN 978-0-500-29135-1

Printed and bound in Malaysia by C.S. Graphics

To find out about all our publications, please visit
www.thamesandhudson.com.
There you can subscribe to our e-newsletter,
browse or download our current catalogue,
and buy any titles that are in print.

The photographs in *The Way We Live* series of books are the result of many years of travelling around the world to carry out commissions for various publications.
Very special thanks is due to Catherine de Chabaneix, for all her help during the production of this book, and for her ongoing commitment to Gilles' remarkable archive.
In addition, thanks to all the people who have helped to make the realization of this project possible, including Martine Albertin, Béatrice Amagat, Catherine Ardouin, Françoise Ayxandri, Marion Bayle, Jean-Pascal Billaud, Anna Bini, Marie-Claire Blanckaert, Barbara Bourgois, Marie-France Boyer, Marianne Chedid, Alexandra D'Arnoux, Jean Demachy, Emmanuel de Toma, Geneviève Dortignac, Jérôme Dumoulin, Marie-Claude Dumoulin, Lydia Fiasoli, Jean-Noel Forestier, Marie Kalt, Françoise Labro, Anne Lefèvre, Hélène Lafforgue, Catherine Laroche, Nathalie Leffol, Blandine Leroy, Marianne Lohse, Véronique Méry, Chris O'Byrne, Christine Puech, José Postic, Nello Renault, Daniel Rozensztroch, Elisabeth Selse, Suzanne Slesin, Caroline Tiné, Francine Vormèse, Claude Vuillermet, Suzanne Walker, Rosaria Zucconi and Martin Bouazis.

Our thanks also go to those who allowed us access to their houses and apartments: Jean-Marie Amat, Mea Argentieri, Avril, Claire Basler, Bébèche, Luisa Becaria, Dominique Bernard, Dorothée Boissier, Carole Bracq, Susie and Mark Buell, Michel Camus, Laurence Clark, Anita Coppet and Jean-Jacques Driewir, David Cornell, Bertile Cornet, Jane Cumberbatch, Geneviève Cuvelier, Ricardo Dalasi, Anne and Pierre Damour, Catherine Dénoual, Dominique and Pierre Bénard Dépalle, Phillip Dixon, Ann Dong, Patrice Doppelt, Philippe Duboy, Christian Duc, Jan Duclos Maïm, Bernard Dufour, Explora Group, Flemish Primitives, Michèle Fouks, Pierre Fuger, Massimiliano Fuksas, Teresa Fung and Teresa Roviras, Henriette Gaillard, Jean and Isabelle Garçon, John MacGlenaghan, Fiora Gondolfi, Annick Goutal and Alain Meunier, Murielle Grateau, Michel and Christine Guérard, Yves and Michèle Halard, Hotel Le Sénéchal, Hotel Samod Haveli, Anthony Hudson, Ann Huybens, Patrick T'Hoft, Igor and Lili, Michèle Iodice, Paul Jacquette, Hellson, Jolie Kelter and Michael Malcé, Amr Khalil, Dominique Kieffer,

Kiwayu Safari Village, Lawrence and William Kriegel, Philippe Labro, Karl Lagerfeld, François Lafanour, Nad Laroche, Rudolph Thomas Leimbacher, Philippe Lévèque and Claude Terrijn, Marion Lesage, Lizard Island Hotel, Luna, Catherine Margaretis, Marongiu, Mathias, Valérie Mazerat and Bernard Ghèzy, Jean-Louis Mennesson, Ilaria Miani, Anna Moï, Leonardo Mondadori, Jacqueline Morabito, Christine Moussière, Paola Navone, Christine Nicaise, Christian Neirynck, Jean Oddes, Catherine Painvin, John Pawson, Christiane Perrochon, Phong Pfeufer, Françoise Pialoux les Terrasses, Alberto Pinto, Stéphane Plassier, Morgan Puett, Bob Ramirez, Riad Dar Amane, Riad Dar Kawa, Yagura Rié, Guillaume Saalburg, Holly Salomon, Jérôme-Abel Séguin, Jocelyne and Jean-Louis Sibuet, Siegrie and her cousins, Valérie Solvi, Taprone Villa, Patis and Tito Tesoro, Richard Texier, Jérôme Tisné, Doug Tomkins, Anna and Patrice Touron, Christian Tortu, Armand Ventilo, Véronique Vial, Barbara de Vries, Thomas Wegner, Quentin Wilbaux, Catherine Willis.
Thanks are also due to the following magazines for allowing us to include photographs originally published by them: *Architectural Digest* (French Edition), *Atmosphère*, *Coté Sud*, *Elle*, *Elle à Table*, *Elle Décoration*, *Elle Décor Italie*, *Madame Figaro*, *Maison Française*, *Marie Claire*, *Marie Claire Idées*, *Marie Claire Maison*, *The World of Interiors*.